the **Ferret**

A guide to selection, housing, care,
nutrition, behaviour, health, breeding,
species and colours

Contents

Foreword

If you're planning to buy an animal, it's important to
get plenty of information well in advance, even if your
preference is for a small animal like the ferret. Is the
animal right for your family? How much work is associated with caring for it, and how much will that cost?
Can you cuddle it or only view it from a safe distance?
This book will give you an overview about the origins
of the ferret, feeding, care, reproduction and the most
common ailments and problems with ferrets. It is also
intended to be a guideline for the responsible buying
and keeping of ferrets.

In this book, you will find practical basic information
about the ferret. For example, where is the best place
to get a ferret? How big does its cage need to be and
what toys are suitable for a ferret? Against which
diseases must a ferret be vaccinated and where can you
find a vet who is specialised in ferrets? You will also
find information about a ferret's behaviour and upbringing.

Ferrets are true social animals and they are best not
kept alone. They are always playful and curious and
need a lot of attention every day. Remember that a well
cared for ferret can live to the age of eight to ten. So
never buy a ferret on the spur of the moment. Think
about the consequences in advance. Do you have space
for a roomy ferret cage? Will ferrets get on with other
pets you may have? If you know what you're letting
yourself in for, ferrets can be fine, playful housemates,
both for you and for your children.

About Pets

A Publication of About Pets.

Co-publisher United Kingdom
Kingdom Books
PO9 5TL, England

ISBN 1852792124
First printing
September 2003

Original title: *de Fret*
© 2000 - 2002 Welzo Media Productions bv,
About Pets,
Warffum, the Netherlands
http://www.aboutpets.info

Photos:
Rob Dekker, Rob Doolaard,
Eeg Manders, Evelien van Veldhuizen,
the Strijk family, C. Stephan,
Barbara van Haaren, Fleur Tenwolde,
J.A. van der Linde and Isabelle Francois

Printed in Italy

In general

At first sight, a ferret could be described as a cross between a puppy, a kitten and a toddler.

Ferrets love to burrow and rummage, and are full of mischief. They are extremely curious, and obey only when it suits them. Most ferrets are kept as companions. Their enormous playfulness (which lasts their whole lives) makes them pleasant housemates. Some people also keep ferrets to hunt with. This method of hunting (for rabbits for example) is called ferreting and is particularly popular in England.

A closer look at the ferret

A ferret is a small animal with a pointed snout, small ears that lie flat to its head, beady eyes, a slender body and a long, thin tail. To some extent the ferret's build resembles that of the the rat, but they are definitely not related. Its Latin name is Mustela putorius furo and it's a member of the marten family (stoat, weasel, badger, polecat and otter). Contrary to popular belief, the ferret is not a rodent. It's more closely related to a dog than to a mouse! A male ferret is called a 'hob' and a female a 'jill'. A young ferret is called a 'kit'.

History

Where and when the ferret was first domesticated (kept as a pet) is a subject of considerable debate. We don't even know exactly where and when cats and dogs were first domesticated, although we know a lot more about them in general. The very first mention of ferrets is to be found in the Book of Leviticus (1000 BC) and in the works of the Greek poet Aristophanes (445 – 338 BC), but we can't be sure if these actually referred to ferrets or to some other member of the marten family. What we do know is that the ancient Greeks knew ferrets, but didn't keep them as domestic animals. They described the ferret as a North African animal with the look of an albino (colourless with red eyes). At that time they were already very tame and lived in people's houses. Nowadays, the Berbers in North Africa still use ferrets in the same way as the Greeks described back then. But it is impossible to say whether the ferret actually originated in this region.

Another unanswered question is which animal was the ancestor of the ferret we know today, because the ferret is an animal that is never found in the wild. This also means that a ferret cannot survive in the wild. Although it's a predator by nature, after killing its prey it has no idea what to do with it.

Because people have always fed it, it does not occur to a ferret that it can actually eat its prey.

It is assumed that the ferret came about through the crossing of the European polecat and the Asian Steppe polecat. As we already have mentioned, the ferret is a member of the marten family, which also includes the polecat. A family tree can be used to see approximately how developments occurred, but unfortunately we don't know exactly how the last step happened, when the ferret actually became distinct from the polecat.

An important part of the ferret's history is ferreting. Through the centuries there have been reports of rabbit-hunting with the aid of ferrets. That the Romans did this

is certain. In fourteenth century England it was the law that only people with an income greater than forty shillings a year were permitted to keep ferrets. This was to prevent the working classes from hunting for highly prized rabbit meat.

A ferreter is still often regarded as a secret poacher, out in the dark of the night with one or more blood-thirsty ferrets. Maybe this picture was once correct, but today ferreters are respectable members of society, who are usually invited by landowners to help them keep the rabbit population on their land under control. If you want go ferreting, you must first find out if it's permitted. In some areas, there may be restrictions or a permit may be required. You also need the permission of the landowner.

Behaviour

Ferrets don't speak a language like humans. But even if they can't talk, they can communicate with each other.

They mostly express their feelings and intentions through various non-verbal communications, to a lesser extent through sounds. A very important part of their communication with each other is play.

Character

Ferrets are active animals. They regularly change their own surroundings. Cloths, food and drink containers and the toilet box are dragged around from one place to another. If they get the chance, it won't only be your home, but too that they'll turn it upside down. Ferrets love to investigate things, and they'll break all your house-rules. This may give the impression that they're stupid and don't understand what they're supposed to do, but in fact, the opposite is

the case: they understand only too well what the intention is. What they do is wait until you give up, so they can go their own sweet way. You can keep this urge to explore under control by playing on their talent to 'navigate', because ferrets love a maze with lots of twists and turns. You can read how you can easily make one in the chapter on "Housing". The stubborn character of the ferret is also apparent when you try to train it. Most people fail to train a ferret to do anything, because they're not consistent enough. A ferret will only do something if, in return, it gets something it enjoys. If you want to train it to do its business in the litter box, then you must always reward it when it does so. Positive experiences are extremely impor-

tant in the learning process. In the long term you can certainly train a ferret to do things, but if you stop rewarding it too early, it will simply give up. This is not because it's unwilling, but because its natural curiosity quickly distracts it.

Senses

The ferret's behaviour sometimes seems difficult to explain, but a little insight into its senses may clarify a thing or two.

Eyes

A ferret only relies on its eyesight to a limited extent. Ferrets' eyes work best in twilight, when the slit-shaped pupil emphasises the outline of potential prey. In the case of predators that hunt animals that move horizontally, the slit-shaped pupil is placed vertically. On the ferret, which usually hunts hopping prey, the pupil is slanted horizontally. It can hardly recognise colours, but it can judge depths and is sometimes even scared of heights. The ferret recognises its housemates not by their appearance, but by their movements, their sounds and their scent.

Ears

New-born ferrets are totally deaf until they're about a month old. That explains the din they make in

the nest: they can't hear themselves. A ferret can hear sounds in the frequency range between 40 Hz and 44 kHz (the maximum a dog can hear). They hear sounds between eight and twelve kHz best, which is why they react so strongly to whistling sounds. Although its almost impossible to observe, ferrets always move their ears in the same way. They always point them towards the source of a sound.

Scents

Scents are even more important for a ferret than for a dog or cat. A ferret can get a lot of information from a scent that has been left somewhere, like the sex and

age of the animal that left it, and whether this may be a potential mate. With its sense of smell, a ferret can determine whether the territory it's in has already been claimed. The ferret also uses its own scent as a diversionary tactic when under attack, hoping this will give it a chance to escape. Ferrets that don't know each other will first sniff and lick each other's hindquarters, and then sniff each other's neck. The ferret's ears also seem to contain a lot of scent information: try letting a ferret sniff at a Q-tip with the earwax of another ferret that it doesn't know.

The importance of play

Omnivores, grazing animals and predators all play in the wild. This is not just good fun for young animals, but highly important. By playing they learn how to behave in relation to their environment. In other words, it is preparation for adulthood. In their play, young animals learn how to fight, hunt and mate, where and when they can find food, and what their place is within the social structure around them. During their games they experience togetherness and security. So it's extremely important that ferrets have contact with other ferrets from an early age. Ferrets that grow up alone can't learn what play is, and they will later be unable to relate normally to other ferrets. Scientific research has shown that ferrets kept with their own kind react without

fear to new situations and unknown objects. Newcomers are welcomed without reservation, and immediately invited to play. A ferret that has grown up alone, on the other hand, will be extremely nervous in new situations, and will never really get used to them. It will try to avoid contact with other ferrets by hiding away. Adult loners often react aggressively towards other ferrets: they launch a kind of preventive attack (if I don't get him first, he'll get me).

Forms of play

The first thing that strikes you when ferrets play is the strange way they move. They stagger jerkily around the whole room. To a layperson they may appear drunk or crazy, but there's nothing at all abnormal about it.

The "War dance of the Weasel"

Ferrets invite each other to play by pestering. They simply jump on top of one another. But the phenomenon that ferret-lovers call the war dance of the weasel is more striking. This is sometimes even observed in ferrets that live alone, where it represents an urge for movement or a form of letting off steam. At first sight, this dance seems to involve the ferret staggering around the room out of control, but nothing could be further from the truth. It starts with the ferret standing upright in front of its selected playmate. Then it

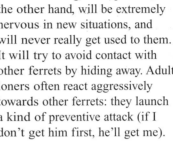

Five games

There are five different forms of a ferret's play:
1. The fight or so-called aggressive play. This is a favourite for both hobs and jills.
2. The chase. This is only played where there's enough room.
3. The hunt, where even dominant or submissive ferrets switch the roles of hunter and prey.
4. Games with objects are played by both sexes (hiding things away).
5. 'Mother and child'. This is almost only played by unsterilised females.

shows its 'open-jaws' look, and jumps in the air with all four paws, or jumps from its forepaws to its rear paws. Meanwhile, it makes twisting movements in the air and shakes its head furiously from side to side. The ferret will usually perform three to five jumps in a row. If it loses sight of its playmate during all this, it will stop and seek eye contact again. If the other ferret also reacts with a war dance, a rough game starts and the animals roll around and fight. If there's no reaction the ferret will repeat the war dance or jump on the other animal. If there are more than two ferrets, the game may be resumed with another, perhaps more willing playmate.

This behaviour appears strange to people when they see it for the first time. Ferrets fall and bump against everything in sight during their war dance; they seem to have gone totally mad. But it's just the normal method ferrets use to get other ferrets interested in playing. You can actually provoke it yourself by waving your hand or a cloth from side to side in front of your ferret. You can also lay the animal on its back, tickle it a little and then stop.

A ferret won't always respond to a companion's invitation. It shows its lack of enthusiasm by not turning to the other animal when "attacked", or by trying to get away. A ferret that doesn't want to play sometimes makes a hissing sound or reacts with an open-mouthed threat. However, ferrets are very stubborn and won't accept a refusal easily. They keep pestering until the other animal accepts or makes it very plain that it's had enough.

It's remarkable that ferrets will adapt the boisterowness of their play to the reactions of their playmate, but they have to learn to do

this: young ferrets are sometimes a little too wild, but they calm down somewhat as they get older. Adapting their play to their playmate usually (but not always) prevents them from hurting or frightening the other animal. This means that bigger, heavier males can play with small toddlers without the little one coming to any harm. A ferret will also adapt its play with a human in line with the way you play with it. If you play wildly with your ferret, it in turn will play rough and tumble with you too.

Most ferrets love fight games. They also love a tug-of-war or a game of hide-and-seek. They love to discover new things and sniff at anything and everything. They also love to drag away and hide your things. Somewhat older females spend most of their time dragging their toys from one hideaway to the next. They love to follow each other around, and once in a while play hunting games together.

Posture and movements

A ferret has a very varied vocabulary of body language. You can learn a lot from its posture and movements. Ferrets communicate with each other using posture and movements more than with sounds. In fact they're very quiet animals. The sounds they do make (in all tones) are primarily 'talking to themselves'. Let's look at a few body postures and movements, so

that you get an idea of what makes a ferret tick.

Quietly walking and looking around: Your ferret wanders into the room. It walks around aimlessly with its little head up, looking at everything. You can see it thinking: 'What can I chew on to get some attention?'

Slow motion: Your ferret moves around very slowly, with its head down and body close to the ground. This is a sign that it's planning to escape unnoticed, almost as if it thinks it can make itself invisible. After all, it's the fast vertical movements that get the attention of other ferrets.

Hunched-up posture: When a ferret is tired and actually should sleep, but is afraid it might miss something, it will sit hunched-up. It will also adopt this posture if it's caught doing something it shouldn't. Then it will heave a sigh, hunch up and stare at you as if you weren't there.

Nibbling and licking: A ferret will do this with its companions but also with people. It will nibble at your finger without really opening its mouth, and give you little licks now and then. This is a sort of 'making up' behaviour. A hob will do the same to get around the jill. But it can also be a sign of unrest and frustration, a kind of 'leave me alone, I've got other things to do' statement.

Ploughing through the carpet: A

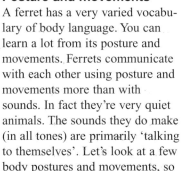

ferret will usually prefer carpet, but will also take pleasure in parquet, shoes or other objects. It will push its nose in as far as it will go, and will push itself through the material with its hind legs. It will often move backwards and forwards. This behaviour is common to all marten types; with the scent glands under their chin

they are marking their territory.

Getting attention: A ferret will regularly try to get your attention by rattling its water bottle or shak-ing the bars of its cage. Sometimes it will do this out of boredom, but at other times it may be trying to point something out to you; perhaps its water bottle is empty. When your ferret does this, very calmly look to see what's up. If you come quickly, it may think its action worked, and it will keep doing it all the time.

The prod: A ferret will do this to signal that it's had enough of its companion's attention. It will prod the other ferret on the neck or shoulder with its nose. They sometimes also do this in an area where they don't want other ferrets at that moment. They're drawing a line: 'thus far, but no further'. A ferret will also sometimes make a pushing movement with its neck arched against another ferret. This is a half-hearted challenge to fight: the ferret wants to fight, but it's not quite sure it can win the fight.

Fear and doubt: Attack? The ferret lies flat on the floor and makes a yapping or barking sound. This is a frightened reaction in response to a threat. The ferret won't bite yet, but it's ready to.

Defensive threat: The ferret, its back arched, stands facing the direction of the threat. Usually its tail is raised. This posture is a sign that the ferret doesn't want to fight, but will defend itself fiercely if it has to. If the threat remains, it will show its open jaws and make a screaming noise. If that doesn't help either, it will go into action.

The bushy tail: This is often produced by fear, but can also be a sign of excitement or ecstasy. Older ferrets love you to scratch their neck and you can sometimes see the hair on its tail, neck and back stand up.

Spread-out toes: Spread-out toes can be a sign of a ferret's feeling of great satisfaction with its lot. Just as a dog wags its tail and a cat purrs, a ferret spreads out its toes. With its eyes closed, it stretches out its forepaws and toes as wide as it can. If a ferret does this

while you're holding it, you can be sure it's enjoying it. But if a ferret stretches out its hind legs and toes at the same time, this is more a sign of stress.

Wagging tail: This is a sign of nervous expectation and tension. The ferret moves its tail from side to side for a few seconds. This is often seen when its head is hidden under something.

Licking ears: When a mother ferret does this with her young, this is a disciplinary measure. In other cases it's a method to make up to another ferret that's higher up in the hierarchy.

Compulsive licking: Females often do this in season or in phantom pregnancy. Ferrets not in season or phantom pregnancy do it as an alternative to biting: One ferret pushes another to the ground and starts to lick it. After the licking, the ferret will often suddenly bite the other animal.

Friendship

Ferrets build close friendships with one another. They show this by licking each other and caring for each other's coat. They hate being separated and become nervous or even go into total panic.

Older ferrets can be very upset when another ferret dies. They may even become aggressive and start biting people. Unfortunately, there's not much you can do. Give it the chance to bid farewell to the corpse of its dead friend, and later put another ferret in the cage. Despite this though, it can sometimes happen that 'deserted' ferrets let themselves go completely and soon die themselves.

Ferrets also have a certain relationship with people. This may not only be friendship, but also can be dislike. When a ferret makes it clear that it doesn't want anything to do with a certain person, this may be because of bad treatment in the past, but may also be scent-related. However odd it sounds, ferrets can be sensitive to the soap or deodorant you use. They can also hate the smell of cigarette smoke.

A ferret will intuitively feel whenever you're feeling down. It will invite you to play. It may even come and get you when another ferret is chewing something it shouldn't, or is in difficulties. A ferret that's got lost or has other problems will never let you know itself (except very young animals). This harks back to the behaviour of their counterparts in the wild, such as the polecat. If they call for help in the wild, there's a chance a predator will treat it as an invitation. So they quietly wait for help. However, if they are in pain, they will make noises!

Biting

Ferrets are not aggressive animals, but they are used to using their teeth. They do with their mouth what we do with our hands. So a ferret will use its teeth in play.

But you have to teach it not to bite, and punish it if it goes too far. Grab it by the scruff of its neck (literally) while you reprimand it. Making a blowing or hissing sound also helps; ferrets do this among themselves if they're angry. If it keeps biting, put it back in its cage as a punishment and ignore it for five minutes or so.

Some people punish their ferret with a tap on the nose. If you do this, remember the following: your ferret may interpret this tap as play and try again, because it thinks you're now playing with it. And for beginners, it's not easy to judge the force of such a tap, and you can easily hurt your ferret! So never tap it on the nose, but always on its side, which it will understand as punishment. Another solution is to 'bite back' by pinching its cheek with your fingers, but the 'scruff of the neck' is still the best punishment.

If your ferret does bite hard and then refuses to let go, try holding it under the tap. It will usually then let go. If it doesn't you're going to have to literally wrench its jaws open. Should your ferret have a tendency to always bite in the same place, rub something on that spot that will repel it (a bitter or sharp taste). Don't forget to reward your ferret if it licks your hand instead of biting it. A reward does not need to be edible. It can be anything your ferret enjoys.

Of course, it's better not to teach a ferret bad habits at the beginning. Certainly don't start playing with it if it's hanging on to your trouser legs. It will find that terrific and will repeat the exercise again and again!

It can happen that your ferret only bites strangers, or only people who don't keep ferrets themselves. In that case you have to 'train' your visitors. Your ferret will only notice that someone new has come in. It will want to 'test' this newcomer, and perhaps even get a taste of them. If it also senses fear, then it will definitely want a bite. Ferrets tend to bite frightened or nervous people. This behaviour will quickly disappear if your visitor doesn't appear frightened, but grabs your animal by the scruff of the neck if it tries to bite. If your visitor is still afraid, it's best to put the ferret back in its cage.

It's human to poke a finger through the wires of a cage to entice or tease a ferret. On the other hand it's typical of a ferret to bite the finger; forbidding it won't help at all. So try to get a ferret used to 'moving parts' in its cage. You can do this by rubbing your finger with something it doesn't like. In the end, it will accept the finger without biting. A mistreated or ill ferret may

deliberately bite itself out of fear or in pain. Naturally punishment is not the answer here. You must be patient until the ferret learns to trust you, and in case of an ill animal, go straight to the vet's.

Walking your ferret

You can go for walks with your ferret on a lead. Most ferrets love to go out on a tour of discovery this way. There are special harnesses for ferrets in pet shops. The best are in a figure of eight. A little bell on its harness will tell you

where your ferret is in the event that it actually does get away, and a container with your address or a tag with your phone number is a good idea too.

Take plenty of time for such a walk. You will probably be stopped by surprised and curious people every few yards.

Buying a ferret

Not everybody is suited to keeping a ferret as a pet. And, with bad upbringing, not every ferret is suitable as a pet.

A ferret that has been in people's hands from early on can be a affectionate and loyal companion. But not all ferrets like a cuddle. They all have their own character.

Ferrets stay playful up to an old age. But caring for them is intensive work. They need a lot of attention and must be let out of their cage at least twice a day.

An important (and not always pleasant) aspect of ferrets is their body odour. Not everyone can take it. Usually, ferrets that have not been treated (and especially the males) can spread a strong smell. But this disappears to a large extent when they're treated. You can read more about that in the chapter 'Caring for your ferret'.

Many people come face to face with a ferret for the first time in a pet shop or at a show, and fall in love at first sight. This often results in an impulse purchase, which ends in a fiasco for both sides. The new owner has no idea how to care for and bring up a ferret, and is quickly disappointed. The ferret then finally winds up in an animal shelter or ferret rescue (if it's lucky).

If you're thinking of getting ferrets, think about it carefully and get plenty of information. After reading this small book, it's a good idea to visit somebody who keeps ferrets, or to look after somebody else's ferret for a while. You'll soon know whether or not a ferret is the right pet for you.

It's also advisable to get information from a vet in advance regarding vaccinations and sterilisation, and the associated costs. Also consider that you must buy a cage (with furnishings), food and toys. Work out how much these items will cost, so you're not faced with unpleasant (financial) surprises later. The better prepared you are, the more pleasure you'll get from your ferrets.

Where to buy a ferret

A pet shop is not always the best place to buy a ferret. First look at

the impression the shop makes. Never do business if the ferrets are not house-trained, and are only seldom handled. Just like a good breeder, a good pet shop should be able to give you correct information, and will also ask you the right questions to check whether you're a suitable person to keep ferrets. Check how the ferrets are housed. Are the cages clean? The floor should not be covered with sawdust, hay, straw or wood chips, but there should be cloths in one corner and a litter box with cat litter. Do the ferrets have clean water (no milk!) to drink in a drinking bottle? Do they have food (ferret food)? If kits are picked up, they may bite, but it shouldn't be a strong bite. If you can't pick the ferret up, for whatever reason, then definitely don't buy it, however hard that decision may be. All in all, the best place to buy a ferret is from a private ferret-lover; they will have looked after their ferrets and can give you all the information and tips you need.

Young or adult?

Of course, young ferrets look sweet, but they need even more attention than adult animals. The advantage is that you can bring up a kit in your own way. If you do buy a young ferret, never buy one that's younger than eight weeks. If a young ferret is separated from its mother too early, this will have disastrous effects later. Never buy

---

Pros and cons of the ferret

Pros
- They spend most of the day in their cage
- They're house-trained by nature
- They're not too big
- They're easy to handle
- They don't eat a lot
- They're pretty, playful and intelligent
- They can get quite old

Cons
- They can stink if not treated
- They have sharp teeth
- Cage must be cleaned every day
- They must be vaccinated every year
- They need a roof over their head, toys and food
- Vet's bills can be expensive
- It can be difficult to find someone to look after them when you go on holiday

a kit without having seen its mother. If you're happy with an adult ferret, get in touch with a ferret club or foundation. You can find some addresses at the back of this book. Almost all these clubs have a ferret shelter or placing service. These are for ferrets that have been put out of their homes, possibly because of disappointment after (impulse) purchase. The clubs place kits and co-ordinate supply and demand for young (especially in the summer) and adult ferrets.

Male or female?

Although there's usually no difference in the price, there are some differences between males and females. A male is not only larger than a female, but differs in behaviour and character too; females are usually more temperamental. Other costs can also differ: sterilisation of a female is more expensive than castrating a male. If you're planning to breed, then a female or a pair (not brother and sister!) is obviously the best choice. In the end, it's all down to personal choice.

One or more?

It's definitely best to keep at least two ferrets. The company of their own kind makes ferrets happy and sociable animals. They can play together and are easy to handle, and taking care of two is no more work than looking after one. Bringing a new ferret into the home usually presents no pro-

blems, or very few. Ferrets usually get on well together. If they fight at first, just keep an eye on them (as long as no blood flows). A pecking order has to be established. You can happily keep males and females together, as long as they're treated before they become adult and sexually mature.

Before you introduce a newcomer, make sure that its vaccinations are all in order. Keep the newcomer apart in another cage and swap the cloths the animals sleep on from one cage to the other, so that they get used to each other's scent. You can also wash your ferrets before introducing the newcomer, then they will all have a neutral scent. Give the newcomer the chance to quietly explore the new environment on its own, so that it knows its way around. The first time you bring the ferrets together should be somewhere they've never been before. This will distract them and avoid fights for territory. They will probably get to know each other peacefully, but keep an eye on them. If a serious fight does develop, you'll have to separate the combatants. In some cases two ferrets might really not be able to stand each other. Bad experiences a ferret has had in the past can play a major role here and, in this case, there's no point in trying to keep them together.

Ferrets and other pets

Ferrets and rabbits, or other small animals or rodents, do not go well

together. After all a ferret is, and will always remain, a predator. A ferret won't be aggressive towards dogs and cats, but it's more likely that they won't accept the ferret. Ferrets are easier to keep with cats than with dogs. Ferrets will usually run behind a cat and playfully bite its heels. A cat will normally just withdraw haughtily. Let your ferret and cat get used to each other by holding them together and letting them sniff each other.

The combination of ferret and dog is a little more problematic. Ferrets love to pester and play, and many a dog won't appreciate that. There are countless tales of ferrets and dogs that get on like a house on fire, but just as many of dogs that have seriously injured or killed ferrets. To reduce the risk to a minimum, be extremely careful. Try to prevent trouble between them as far as possible.

Ferrets and children

Ferrets and children can become great pals, but the presence of an adult is a must, especially in case of younger children. They can hurt a ferret by pinching it too enthusiastically. The ferret, in turn, can also administer a nasty bite.

Children under twelve should not be allowed to care for ferrets on

their own. The cage must be cleaned every day, and ferrets need to run free at least twice a day. In other words, caring for ferrets is always intensive work. Young children can't take this responsibility alone but, helped by an adult, they can gradually learn how to care for an animal, and how to handle it with care. Do remember though that robust handling of a ferret can provoke an equally robust response on the animal's part.

Home at last

Whatever ferret you've bought (a kit, adult, from a ferret shelter, from a private person or a pet shop), you'll be happy to get it home. In your enthusiasm, of course, you'd like to cuddle it and show it everything. But remember that the ferret is probably anxious after the journey home. Let it sort itself out first. Put it in the middle of the living room (or the room it can later run in) and leave it in peace. Let the ferret explore the room at its own pace and don't pick it up. Leave its cage open and let it go where it wants. If it looks like it might do its business, put it in its litter box.

Don't start playing with your ferret at once (unless it invites you to) and don't let the other ferrets loose yet. Give your new friend the chance to get used to its new situation. If you do things too hastily, there's a chance it will bite out of nervousness, or behave badly in some other way. It is interested in everything, but also frightened. A ferret will need several weeks to get used to its new situation and its new owner. Don't be disappointed too early; if your new ferret bites hard on the first day, it can still become the most affectionate ferret ever within a couple of weeks.

Housing your ferrets

Ferrets are most comfortable in a large cage, and they need to be able to run around freely in a room twice a day.

A ferret cage must be at least 100x60x60 cm, but preferably as big as possible. Cages of this size are very expensive to buy in a pet shop, but you don't have to be a master builder to make one yourself.

Do-it-yourself
The start of a good ferret cage is a floor-plate of a smooth, water-proof material that won't absorb urine. Wood is not suitable. Ferrets love to climb, so a high cage with various floors is ideal. Make sure it's sturdy, because a ferret loves a hefty romp. Make the rear and one or both side panels closed; wire or gauze is the best for the front. Make sure that ventilation is good, but also that the cage is 'escape-proof', because ferrets are true escape artists. Not every ferret will turn

its cage upside down to see if it can get out, but some make it a sport to always be coming up with new surprises for their owner.

The best place
You can keep ferrets indoors or out. The advantage of keeping them outdoors is that you're not subjected to that oh-so-special ferret odour. But in practice, ferrets kept outdoors often seem to get forgotten, and receive too little attention. A place indoors, near people, is preferable.

Ferrets don't like it hot.
Temperatures of more than 28° C are too high, so never put the cage directly in the sun. Ferrets must never be kept in a glass container, such as an old aquarium, because temperatures can quickly soar in it.

If it does get really hot, give your ferrets a cool-down with water, a fan (not too close to the cage, and switch it off regularly), wet stones or wet cloths. Avoid placing cold objects, like a jug of ice-cubes, directly next to their body. A ferret can't handle that. Always ensure your ferrets can't catch a cold.

Cage litter
A bare floor in its cage isn't a problem for a ferret. Indeed, it's ideal because otherwise it will regard its whole cage as a huge toilet. If you really want to use some kind of cage litter, then never use sawdust, hay, straw or wood chippings. Ferrets have sen-

sitive bronchial tracts and the dust in these materials can make them seriously ill. Resinous wood products give off fumes, which can bother many ferrets. What they will enjoy is cloths or old T-shirts to sleep on.

The interior
A ferret cage must be functional but equipped with lots of interesting objects. Indispensible are a night hutch, toys, a litter box, food container and water bottle. Ferrets like to sleep in a night hutch or a hammock, with an old sweater or T-shirt. This bedding should be washed regularly to prevent it from smelling. Ferrets are mad

about hammocks, and you can easily make these yourself. Give them their food in a sturdy container which is weighted down or fixed in place, otherwise they will be sure to drag it around! Give water in a big water bottle (as for rabbits). To prevent your ferrets from moving all the furniture around all the time, items can be fixed to the cage with strips of wire or something similar.

Toys

Ferrets love to play and can't live without toys. Of course, you can buy things in pet shops, but you can just as easily make them yourself very cheaply. Here are a few suggestions:

• Fill a large cardboard box with cellophane, shredded paper or small balls, and cut a few openings in the sides.

• Fix Perspex to the four sides of an old playpen. Fill it with sand, with a drainage pipe here or there. You can also use a large plastic container or mortar tub.

• Take PVC pipes wide enough for your ferrets to run through. Make a maze using U-bends and T-connectors. Make sure you change it regularly, as this will keep your ferrets curious and alert.

• Lay a folded cloth or a pillowcase on the floor and fill it with cellophane. Your ferrets will love to dance on this because it makes such a splendid sound.

• Hang a rope flowerpot holder about thirty centimetres high and hang a towel from it.

• Fill a bathtub or bowl with ten centimetres of water and put a few small balls in it. Make sure your ferrets can climb in and out of the water. Always supervise this game!

• Make a slide, for example from a bench to the floor, with a wide diameter PVC pipe.

• Take your ferrets with you when you make the bed. They love to tunnel under the bedclothes and between the pillows.

• Stuff some toys into a big paper bag; this will provide hours of fun.

• Change toys regularly. This makes it more interesting for your ferrets, because there's always something new. A ferret is easy to amuse but can quickly get bored. Keep them happy by always giving them new things to play with.

Litter box

Ferrets are clean animals that are happy to do their business in a litter box. Put the box (a cat litter box is ideal) full of cat litter, close to the sleeping area. Ferrets will normally do their business, both big and small, when they wake

up. Choose a cat litter which is neither dusty nor can easily stick together. Because ferrets love to burrow, the litter could quickly clot in their nose, and dust is bad for them too. Pick a litter box with high sides and a low entrance. Ferrets will always go to a back corner to do their business. Make sure the box is firmly fixed in place.

Running free

Ferrets must be able to run free and romp every day. This is not without risks. As we have said, they are exceptionally curious and skilful escape artists. So you must make your house 'ferret-proof'. As soon as you bring a ferret into your home, it will find places you never knew existed! They won't miss any corner, space, chink, crack that they can get into, under or over. Places that might be dangerous, like behind a boiler, fridge, washing machine or drier must be protected with gauze. Even if your ferret can get in, there's no guarantee it can get out again, and if you try to pull it out you may literally pull the wool over its eyes.

If you want to leave doors open, fit them with a sheet of Perspex or wood that is high enough to prevent your ferrets from getting out. Ferrets are experts at opening cupboards, and will pull everything out, so keep them locked. Watch out with sofas and chairs as ferrets can easily get between the

covering and the springs. Take anything fragile out of the room where they play, and also anything made of rubber. Ferrets love to nibble at rubber but it's not good for them. Never underestimate their ability to jump and climb, so keep the toilet-lid shut, don't leave empty buckets around and remove toilet rolls. If a ferret gets its head tangled up in a toilet

roll, it can suffocate! Don't leave plastic bags hanging around. If a ferret nibbles at these it can become very ill. Although it's rare, there are ferrets that like to sample cables and houseplants. This can lead to an electrical shock or poisoning.

Check household equipment (washing machine or drier) before use. There may be a ferret slee- ping inside. Ferrets love to dig more than anything, not only into the carpet, but also into flower pots, so keep these covered with stones or chicken wire.

Nutrition, feeding your ferrets

A ferret must have food and water available, both at night and during the day. Ferrets are predators and therefore 100% carnivorous.

The (closely related) polecat in the wild eats mostly mice, frogs and worms. Ferrets are often fed with cat-food (but don't give them dog biscuits, which don't contain enough nutrients). You can also buy special ferret food. This must contain the following nutrients: 36% (rough) animal protein (dry cat food usually contains 30 - 34%), 20% rough fat and 2% rough cellulose (but certainly not more!). Don't give ferrets fish, it will make their droppings smell even worse.

Try to buy food without colourings and other supplements. Ferrets may be fed canned food, but not too much. Their droppings will become thinner and they may smell.

As an extra treat, they can have a raisin or a small piece of fruit (melon or apple) or vegetables (cucumber, (bell)pepper). Ferrets have a short intestine, which has difficulty digesting plant fibres, so only ever give them very small pieces! They also enjoy vitamin paste but don't give them too much. Ferrets should not eat products containing lactose (such as milk), as these will give them diarrhoea.

One striking characteristic of adult ferrets is that they will never fight over food like most other animals do.

Learning to eat
The young of marten types in the wild learn to recognise the scent of their food at between two and three months. Anything they have

not smelled during this period they will not eat in later life. Their eating behaviour is learned and not in-born.
With young ferrets the limit is at about two months. This explains why many ferrets will only ever eat one thing. During the 'imprinting' period, they never got anything else.

Vitamin preparations

If you feed your ferrets good ferret food, you needn't worry about vitamin or mineral shortages. Ferrets that only get dry cat food or are pregnant, weaning or weakened may very well need multivitamin preparations. There are two sorts on the market that are suitable for ferrets. Ferretone is a vitamin-rich oil-based product, which almost all ferrets are crazy about, but it's not always easy to find. Nutri-cal and Nutri plus are good alternatives, but they contain a lot of sugar and so are not suitable for certain ill animals. Don't give them cat snacks with added vitamins; this would be too much of a good thing for a ferret.

Snacks

Naturally, you'd like to spoil your ferrets once in a while. The above vitamin products are a suitable treat, but in moderation.
On special occasions, you can give your ferrets a great treat with a few raisins or a small piece of fruit or vegetable (not cabbage!). With some experimenting, you can discover what your ferrets like best, but never give them chocolate, crisps, biscuits or sweets! These are bad for their teeth and they can get stomach or intestinal complaints from the salt, fat and sugar these snacks contain.

Caring for your ferrets

If your ferrets are well looked after, people will come to see them.

So they need to be washed now and then, if they've got really dirty. From time to time, their nails must be clipped, and you must bear in mind that ferrets can get fleas too.

Grooming
You don't need to brush a ferret, except during the moulting period, as its hair will always be in good shape. Brushing is recommended during moulting to prevent hairballs forming. You can wash ferrets now and again, although this is not strictly necessary, unless they've used their anal glands to fight off fleas. A ferret's nails must be clipped regularly because they don't wear down on their own. Promote natural wear by taking your ferrets for a walk, giving them bricks to play on, or putting a paving slab in their cage. When you clip their nails, watch out for the 'quick'. This is the pink part of the nail and you should be careful not to cut into it, because this would be painful for the animal and it can bleed copiously. Hold the nail flat while you clip it to avoid splitting.

If your ferret has fleas, you can get rid of them with various products that you can get from your vet.

In the bath
If your ferret does need a bath, use special ferret shampoo or kitten shampoo (because of the acidity). Fill the bath with about 10 centimetres of lukewarm water. Get your ferret nicely wet, rub in the shampoo and then rinse out

the foam properly with clean water. You can then dry the animal off lightly with a towel. Lay a few towels on the floor and let it do its own thing. It's fun watching it rub itself dry. Don't bathe a ferret when it's not necessary. Washing too often can cause skin irritations with all the consequences these have.

That "ferret" smell

The smell of the ferret is a popular topic of discussion. We all know the expression 'stinks like a polecat'. Ferrets can also stink to high heaven, but there are things you can do about it. Many people can't stand the smell of ferrets and have their anal glands removed. This is in fact illegal, because the operation can lead to all kinds of behavioural and health problems. Apart from that, it's not even the anal glands that cause ferrets to smell. A ferret that feels seriously threatened will only empty its anal glands in exceptional cases. This indeed smells awful, but the smell quickly disappears and it is certainly not a reason to have the glands removed.

Fighting the smell:

1. Have the ferret castrated or sterilised.
2. Wash the ferret less often. The more a ferret is washed, the more skin fats it will produce, and the more it will stink.
3. Wash its bedding regularly.

Superfluous skin fats are the main cause of the smell. Ferrets mark their territory in three ways: with urine, with anal secretion (this comes with their droppings) and by rubbing skin fats onto objects. They made their mark by rubbing their belly over an object. Ferrets also display this behaviour when they're bored or really stressed. Males do it more than females, but castrated males and females usually (but not always) smell much less. But the smell is no reason not to keep ferrets in the house. A clean ferret won't smell, even if you hold it to your nose. It's simply a question of cleaning their nest material every day, because their skin fats stick to it. In fact, it's not the ferret that stinks, but its environment. Also remember that an untreated male will deposit drops of urine all over the place during the mating season.

Ears

A ferret produces a lot of earwax. This must be removed regularly. Put a few drops of baby-oil onto a Q-tip. Only clean the visible parts of the ear. Never go into the ear because this will damage the auditory channel. Yellow to reddish-brown earwax is normal. If it's black, then the ferret is suffering with ear mites and must be treated by a vet.

Reproduction

A litter of young ferrets can be an attractive idea. But you need to consider a few things before starting to breed.

If you can't or don't want to keep the young, you have to find good homes for them. Breeding and bringing up a litter of young ferrets has costs attached to it too. If practical problems don't put you off, you need to make sure you've got a suitable pair to mate. Are both male and female in good condition? Do both parents have a nice character? Are you sure they're not related? In-breeding can cause many problems, such as young with in-born defects.

If you have decided to breed a litter, you can allow the female to be covered when she is in season. Jills in season have a swollen genital organ (vulva). If the vulva is not swollen the female is not yet in season, has already mated or is in phantom pregnancy. A

phantom pregnancy lasts 42 days, just as long as a normal pregnancy, but of course no kits are born. Afterwards, the female can go into season normally again.

Once the female is actually pregnant, a number of problems can arise during the pregnancy and after the birth. A female ferret has eight teats, but can bear up to fifteen kits. This will certainly lead to problems during weaning. In some cases a mother may kill her young, in exceptional cases she may even eat them.

Determining the sex
You can see the difference between a male and a female by looking under their belly. If you see a sort of 'navel' (the foreskin), then you have a male. The female has a

second opening below the anus. If you're still in doubt watch them carefully on the litter box. Ferrets always urinate and empty their bowels in one session. Males leave a wet patch a few centimetres in front of their droppings, while females urinate on top of theirs.

The female ferret

A female born around April will go into season for the first time at eight or nine months. But if it's kept indoors or under artificial light this may happen at fifteen weeks! The timing of the first season depends entirely on the lighting situation in its home. To avoid your jills going into season too early, your hobs wanting to mate with everything in sight when they are only five months old, or your older ferrets having problems with hair loss, stick to the following rule: As soon as the sun sets, all your ferrets must be in their cage to sleep.

During the season the vulva (normally just a few millimetres wide) swells rapidly and gives off a musk scent. Then the opening is large and stiff enough to accommodate the male's penis and no semen can escape.

Females in season usually undergo a character change: some become nervous and excited, others soft and lazy. They eat less and their condition deteriorates. If their season lasts too long, they develop a form of anaemia at a certain

moment, also known as bone marrow depression. The female will refuse all food and die.

The only way to save such a female is to have her sterilised immediately. However, sterilisation of a female suffering from serious bone marrow depression is not without risk, so always contact a vet who is a ferret specialist!

A healthy female will never attack a male or escape, except in a playful way. Female ferrets are so built that a male can never force his way in (except by pure luck). The female must co-operate for the mating to succeed. Sometimes a male will hold a female tight for two or three hours without penetrating the vulva. If mating has been successful the male's belly will be wet. If ovulation has taken place the female's vulva will start to shrink back to its normal size within a few days. Almost half of all pregnancies are phantom pregnancies. This is usually caused by a mating session that was too short, mating too late in the year, medical problems (cysts in the Fallopian tube) or in-breeding.

The male ferret

A male becomes an adult once its testicles descend into the scrotum. This happens at the latest during the winter following its birth. A male can best be castrated once it's adult. It will lose some muscle mass, but retains its bulkier bone-structure.

The penis is visible under the belly, six to eight centimetres from the anus. A male ferret does not get an erection. The penis always stays the same size and in the same position. Young males are less suitable for covering a female as their penis is not yet fully developed. An adult male will push its foreskin against the female's vulva so the penis can slide in. On the penis is a sort of 'hook' that keeps the penis inside the female. Young males don't yet have this hook and have to work harder to keep the penis inside the female, increasing the risk of a failed mating. This hook can also lead to accidents. A ferret may get caught on something, causing heavy bleeding or an infection.

Adult non-castrated males should not be kept together in one cage. They can play so rough with each other that they cause injuries. Usually the ferret that is at the top of the hierarchy wins any fight, and it's only over when he's had enough. In addition, a rutting male will try to mate with everything in sight. They leave drops of urine everywhere, which smells awful. If you're not planning to use a male for breeding, it's best to have it castrated as soon as it is sexually mature. At the end of the summer, the male's sexual activity will reduce, its testicles will become smaller and withdraw into his belly.

Mating

The best time for mating is between two and four weeks after the vulva has started to swell. Male and female will court each other as soon as they get the chance. This courting takes about twenty minutes and is similar to normal ferret play. The male ferret is no gallant gentleman and the female does not play a great role in the foreplay. She approaches the male and sniffs him, he then also responds by sniffing. Sometimes the female will push her rear end into his face in invitation. If she's less cautious, she may stand over him.

Usually this is enough to lead to mating. If not, they may carry on playing for a while. After about a quarter of an hour the male will try to find out if the female is ready to mate by grabbing her by the neck. If she's not ready she will try to roll away underneath him. The male will then grab her tightly at the neck. A female ferret in season is often also in two minds. She will attract the male's attention, but if he tries to mate she will try to turn away, or even attack him. As her season goes on, the female becomes less and less fussy. This is a remnant from life in the wild. At the beginning of their season, animals in the wild can decide whether they want to mate with a certain male or not. As time goes by, the need to mate gets stronger and stronger, and they have to be happy with

whatever they get. An unmated female stays in season and can die as a consequence. Inviting various males is also a kind of 'comparing the wares'. It's important that the strongest, most powerful animal provides offspring.

Mating itself can take up to three hours. It's not a particularly romantic interlude. The male will often bite into the female's neck until it bleeds. She needs extended contact to ovulate (some thirty hours after mating).

The male does not ejaculate all at once, but a little every few minutes. The semen has a life expectancy of around 160 hours, and can even still fertilise an egg after another male has mated with the female.

Mating is over once the female tries to separate and come out from under the male. If he doesn't let her go, she will turn on him and bite. If you've had little experience with ferrets, then place the pair in as small a space as possible. This prevents the male dragging the female around more than necessary during mating.

One mating session in the morning and one in the evening should be enough. Keep the animals separated in the meantime so they can regain their strength. Ensure that there is never more than one day between mating sessions, otherwise there's a chance that the kits in the litter may be a few days different in age.

Pregnancy

Most pregnant females will not display any special behaviour until about two weeks before birth. Then they start 'mothering'. This may include them regarding a person (or sometimes another ferret) as their child and they will follow them around trying to lick them. In extreme cases they may fight anyone and everything to keep them away from their surrogate child.

You can pick any place you want for the birth to take place, but the mother-to-be will pick another place if she gets the chance. You can help her as much as possible by doing the following: Make sure that the entrance to the nest at ground level is in the dark. The entrance should preferably be about seven centimetres high and forty centimetres long. The nest must be small inside. Ferrets like to feel something around them on all sides.

About three weeks after mating, the female loses her coat. It is replaced by really thin short fur, so that the kits get as much body-warmth as possible after the birth. It can also happen that ferret mothers run a slight fever (41 °C) for the first three days after the birth, which is also so that they are able to give their young more warmth. During the last 48 hours before the birth, the female is usually quiet and still. As birth approaches she may become very exci-ted and affectionate. Often a female will wait until her favourite person is close-by before giving birth to her young. If she's got a lot of kits in her belly, milk may drip from her teats.

The birth

The first contractions are normally accompanied by a (dark) brown secretion from the vulva. Normally, any kits that have died in the womb during the final stages of pregnancy will arrive first. It can take up to eight hours before the first live kits appear. A jill that is attached to people will enjoy the feel of your hand on her body during contractions. The contractions come in waves, with short and shorter periods between them. They are strongest when a kit comes into position to be pushed out.

During birth, the mother-to-be will usually lie comfortably on her back. If she allows, you can even support her in a sort of sitting position (one hand under her fore-paws, the other under her hind-quarters). This position allows her to sit up on her rear paws. Single kits or twins often cause pro-blems, because they're much big-ger than 'normal' kits (sometimes they weigh twice as much!). As soon as the young are born, the mother will lick them clean and eat the afterbirth.

Sometimes the mother may drag her kits off to the most unlikely places in the house several times a day. Usually these are her favouri-te hideaways. It goes without say-ing that this is not good for the young, so don't give the young mother access to the whole house!

Some mother ferrets are so pro-tective that they won't let anybody near their young. This instinctive behaviour is at its strongest about four days after the birth. It's diffi-cult to predict how this instinct might manifest itself in your fer-ret. If you have a good relationship with her, she may allow you to carefully touch her and her kits. If she protests, leave her in peace. There's a risk she might otherwise kill her young! Make sure no unfamiliar male ferret comes into the house after the birth, because the mother will almost certainly kill her young as soon as she smells him!

With the first litter, the mother may have no milk or may reject her young. Sometimes this may be because someone has touched them, but the usual reason is that the female is still far too young to be a mother. Physically she's able to, but she's not yet mentally mature enough. Never allow a female to mate before she's at least nine months old.

Female ferrets will also help raise the kits of another ferret, as long as the age difference to her own young is not too large. Whenever several mothers in the same cage have young at the same time, they will raise them together. But in the case of simultaneous pregnan-cies there's a big chance that one will give birth a few weeks before the others. They then suffer what amounts to a spontaneous miscar-riage, so that they can help care for the first-born litter. You can avoid this risk by keeping preg-nant females apart until their kits are a little bigger.

Development

A new-born ferret weighs some seven to ten grams and is five to six centimetres long. The build of the young will depend on the con-dition of the mother and the num-ber of young in the litter. Litters of three or less usually don't sur-vive. Moreover mothers with a lit-ter that is too small, may go into season again during weaning. If she can't or won't provide milk for her young, it's an almost impossible task to rear the young yourself.

As soon as a ferret is born, it will draw attention to itself because it's cold. During the first three days of its life it is unable to keep its own body temperature at the right level. These first sounds are crucial to the young ferrets' survival. The mother will abandon kits that don't make a sound for several minutes after their birth. It can also happen that a deaf mother will kill her young because she can't hear their squeals.

The young ferrets don't only depend on their mother for warmth, but also for cooling. They sweat profusely before their fur starts growing. If this happens when their mother is not around, they can literally stick together and die. The sweat of young ferrets stinks to high heaven, by the way, but for good reason. The mother will take anything that carries this scent to the nest. If you were to spread the scent of a young ferret on a cat, the mother ferret would also try to drag the

will start to squeal after a while, and try to find their way into the middle of the little heap of bodies. You can calm loudly complaining kits by breathing warm air over their backs.

Sometimes, for some unknown reason, one of the young won't stay with the group. If the mother didn't retrieve each time, it would die of hypothermia.

After a week, the kit's coats start growing. If the parents were the polecat variety, they will now have a thin dark line around the eyes.

In the second week of their lives, the ferrets' appearance changes substantially, but not their behaviour. They now get their puppy coats. Their weight has now doubled since birth and they're more than twice as long. Their ears start to take shape and stand up from the head. The young can now get up on their forepaws quite quickly and raise their heads, but at the end of the second week they will crawl around like tiny sea lions. They will put everything they can grab straight in their mouths, be it their mother's tail or a part of a brother or sister. The first milk teeth appear at two weeks. After about a week, the mother will put morsels of food in the nest, and the kits will hold them in their paws and start nibbling them. At this age (3.5 weeks) you can also feed the kits gruel

cat to the nest. The mother will not usually let her babies suckle until all the young have been born. The young can survive about twelve hours without their mother's milk. For the first two weeks of their life, they suckle every ninety minutes to two hours. They knead their mother's belly with their paws to get the milk flowing (just like kittens). You can often see brown crusts of dried milk around their mouths and on their paws.

Immediately after birth, the young ferrets are only able to move their forepaws. Together, they form as small a ball as possible in the nest to serve the maximum amount of warmth. The kits on the outside

(nutrilon Soya with rice flour). After about three weeks the young ferrets will make a healthy noise, they can now also make co-ordinated movements and keep crawling out of the nest. Their mother has her hands full. When they're asleep, they appear to be dead. They lay completely still.

At four weeks the young ferrets come out of the nest to go to the litter box (which they find by its scent) and eat any food they find en route. If you want house-trained ferrets, this is the time to get them used to the litter box. Most now have their ears open. Their eyes open on average between the fourth and fifth week. At five weeks they play together and need much more space. Now they should be allowed to let their curiosity and playfulness run wild on any object, as long as it's not dangerous. Ferrets at about seven weeks have double canine teeth. This means that the change of teeth has begun. This lasts about three weeks. The 'adult' teeth are light in colour, the milk teeth are fairly transparent and particularly sharp! As ferrets use their mouths to pick up or move anything they fancy, it's now time for them to learn that you don't have armoured skin, and that they need to be

careful with their teeth. With much patience, love and understanding you'll get there. Now it's also time for them to make acquaintance with the other ferrets in the house, but don't leave them together unsupervised yet. The best age for them to go to a new owner is from eight weeks on. During this period young ferrets may bite or be moody because of the change of teeth. It can sometimes help to soak their food chunks in water.

Castration

Castration is a term that can be used for both sexes. While we say

that a female is 'sterilised', in fact it amounts to castration.

Rendering ferrets infertile is very important. Males are easier to handle following castration, and their smell is reduced by at least eighty percent. Females should be castrated unless you plan to breed with them. A non-treated female continuously produces hormones and, if this continues, she will eventually suffer from bone marrow depression. The best age to have a ferret castrated is between 6 and 9 months.

House-training

Don't be misled by the idea that ferrets are house-trained by nature and don't foul their own nest. This applies only to their sleeping area. On the contrary, ferrets are lazy and if they decide that the litter box is too far away, they may well choose a corner of the living room. House-training for ferrets takes a lot of time and patience. Even if ferrets were house-trained by the breeder, this does not necessarily mean that they will be so in their new home. Their new owner must spend some time observing them and keeping them house-trained.

The most important element in house-training is watching the young ferrets. Put them in the litter box as soon as they wake up. That's usually when they need to go. If, at another time, you notice one of them lifting its tail and

lowering its hindquarters, then it's about to empty its bowels. Put it on the litter box to do its business, and leave it there. Ferrets smell each other's droppings, and it helps them to learn what the right place is.

You can also put some of the cloths they sleep on in front of the litter box. Their scent will help them find the way. If one of them does its business in a place you don't want them to, clean it up immediately, otherwise the others may well follow the example! Keep your ferrets under observation and don't give up too quickly. Rewarding success with a tasty treat or a word of praise will stimulate them and you'll eventually achieve lasting success.

Five golden rules for house-training

1. Fix the litter box firmly in place.
2. Keep your ferrets in a small room until they're house-trained.
3. Keep their litter box and its surroundings well cleaned.
4. Don't use cleaning materials with a sharp smell.
5. Be firm: don't let a ferret out of its cage until it's done its business.

Teaching a ferret not to bite

Normally, kits don't bite, but can sometimes go too far in their enthusiasm for play. And a young ferret has to learn how it can grip you without causing pain. If a ferret bites too hard, make a high sound. That's what they do among themselves if one goes too far. Don't let it go as soon as it bites, as this will teach it that biting means getting away and doing whatever it wants. In the case of a persistent biter, grab it by the scruff of its neck and hold it close to your face. While you blow at its snout, you firmly say "No!". But don't be too rough.

Your ferret's health

A healthy ferret is lively, its eyes are clear and its nose a little moist and cold. Its coat must be soft and glossy.

Its droppings must not be too thin, and its urine bright in colour. Depending on its activity its body temperature ranges between 37.5 and 40° C (average 38.5 - 38.8° C). A healthy ferret breathes about 30 to 40 times a minute, and its heart rate is 160 to 300 beats per minute.

Ill ferrets can show (some of) the following symptoms: apathy, reluctance to play, reduced appetite, dull look, no droppings, swellings and pains in the belly area, lumps, wheezing, loose skin, extreme fur-loss, swollen vulva, fits, diarrhoea, vomiting, constant sneezing in combination with a runny nose, watery eyes and continual coughing.
A common symptom with ferrets is trembling. This is usually no cause for concern. Ferrets tremble when they wake up to get their body temperature to the right level. They also tremble when they're being bathed, when they are excited or frightened. That's the reason why kits often tremble; for them, everything is new and fascinating.

Coat and skin abnormalities
Check the condition of your ferrets' coats regularly. You can check whether your ferrets are in good shape this way. A healthy coat should be glossy, feel soft and fall loosely. A dry, dull and matt coat is a sign that something is not in order. The skin under the coat should be light pink in colour and under no circumstances be irritated, red, moist or scaly. In that case there is a skin condition

that can be caused by parasites, mould, dehydration, skin tumours or certain ailments. A coat that feels dry can also point to a worm infestation, but this is relatively rare in ferrets. In a long season, oestrogen in the bloodstream can cause fur-loss. Even if your ferret does not appear to be really ill, but just 'different to normal', get in touch with your vet. A ferret that has 'something wrong' can go downhill fast!

Vaccination

Ferrets can be plagued not only by visible conditions such as fleas and worms, but are also vulnerable to more serious diseases. The importance of vaccinations cannot be overstated. Ferrets must be vaccinated against distemper and Weil's disease.

Vaccination plan for a ferret
- *At nine weeks:* vaccination against distemper and Weil's disease
- *At fourteen weeks:* Booster vaccinations
- *Thereafter:* Renew annually

If you get an adult ferret that has not been vaccinated as a kit, proceed as follows:
- **As soon as possible:** vaccination against distemper and Weil's disease
- *After three weeks:* Booster vaccinations
- *Thereafter:* Renew annually

Common ailments

There are some diseases and ailments to which a ferret is particularly vulnerable. Let's take a look at them:

Distemper or Carré's Disease

Ferrets are extremely vulnerable to this disease, and must be vaccinated against it. See page 56 for an overview of how to proceed. Carré's disease is caused by the distemper virus. Infection is caused by contact with infected dogs or other ferrets. The disease is practically 100% fatal. Seven to ten days after infection, the ferret loses its appetite, develops a fever and suffers from discharges from eyes and nose. Eczema appears under the chin, around the anus and groin. The condition gradually gets worse, and after two to five weeks the animal dies. Treatment rarely helps, so vaccination is vital!

Rabies

A ferret can transfer the rabies virus to other animals (and humans!) through a bite. The virus is usually in its saliva, but can also be transferred via open wounds. Because ferrets with rabies form a threat to human life they must be put to sleep. Rabies does not exist in the British Isles, so a ferret kept at home runs little risk of rabies, however ferrets that are taken abroad, or imported, must by law be vaccinated against rabies.

can develop into a chronic condition, which ultimately leads to starvation and death. Black, tarry droppings can be a symptom. Aleutian Disease is untreatable. In fact putting an infected animal to sleep is the only way to prevent the virus from spreading.

Weil's Disease

This serious disease is spread by rats' urine and can be fatal for animals and humans. It is absolutely vital to vaccinate ferrets against it!

Waardenburg's Syndrome

This is a genetic defect with, as a result, partial or total deafness, narrow blue or different-coloured eyes that are wide apart and a white stripe that runs from the front to the back of the head. Never buy a ferret with a 'badger stripe'. Even if they're successful in shows, they're totally deaf!

Insulinoma

Insulinoma is caused by small, multiple tumours in the pancreas. These cause a drop in the blood sugar level. In fact it's the opposite of diabetes. The symptoms are general weakness, behaviour changes and muscle deterioration.

Aujeszky's Disease

This disease was originally found in pigs. Infection is caused by eating raw pork or abattoir residue. There is no cure and the disease is fatal, so never give a ferret raw or undercooked pork!

Aleutian Disease

This is a condition caused by a so-called parvovirus (not to be confused with canine parvovirus, which affects dogs). The infection often runs its course unnoticed, but it

Adrenal gland conditions

These conditions are responsible for most deaths of ferrets older than four years. Symptoms are hair-loss, excessive sexual drive, swollen vulva, itching and weight loss.

Cardiomyopathy/ heart conditions

Older ferrets often suffer heart problems. The blood circulation no longer functions properly because of the weakened heart. Fluid accumulation in lungs and belly can be the result.

Ferrets are tough animals and they will usually recover from light illnesses without you noticing. You only notice when things have become a lot worse, and this is sometimes too late. So keep a good eye on your ferrets and be alert for changes in behaviour,

posture and their appearance. It's better to go to the vet for nothing than to go too late!

Other problems
Apart from the diseases and conditions described above, there are a number of other factors that can affect your ferrets' well-being and health.

Stress
A ferret that has to live alone often suffers stress and related

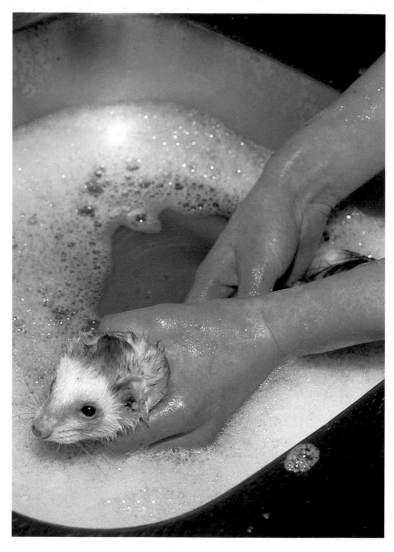

conditions. It often reacts in an exaggerated manner to certain situations to get your attention. It can also be a victim of anxiety attacks.

Blind ferrets often get very attached to a companion and try to maintain constant body contact. If this 'helper' is suddenly gone, they can go into total panic.

Nausea
You can see when a ferret is feeling nauseous. It pulls its stomach up (the sides of the belly become flat and stick out sideways) and/or it scratches its palate with its forepaws. Just like cats, ferrets can have problems with hairballs, but they seldom vomit them out. These hairballs can become so large that they can only be removed surgically.

Nutrient deficiencies
Nutrient deficiencies arise from unbalanced or incorrect feeding. A shortage of vitamin E can lead to infection of fatty tissues, which can cause swellings under the skin. Deficient feeds can also lead to a matt or dry coat or fur-loss.

Fits
Ferrets can also suffer from convulsions, sometimes coupled with loss of consciousness. They can be caused by epilepsy, heat stroke, diabetes, tumours and poisoning (cleaning materials!). Never give a ferret aspirin; it will kill it!

Nicotine addiction
Ferrets who are used to an environment where people smoke can experience withdrawal symptoms after moving to a new home. They can literally get addicted to nicotine! Coversely, ferrets that are not used to tobacco smoke do not feel comfortable in a smoking environment. They may even start to bite.

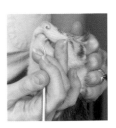

Parasites
Parasites such as (lint)worms, fleas, lice, tics and mites are generally easy to treat. There are various products on the market, but not all are suitable for ferrets. Never administer a cat or dog product on your own initiative, but contact a vet. He should make a diagnosis and prescribe just the right treatment.

The older ferret
A ferret will live eight to ten years, unless it is castrated too young (before 6 months). In that case its life expectancy is substantially less. A ferret at six is thus more or less old, and this is clearly visible. Its winter coat is no longer so thick, it goes grey and is infertile, sleeps more, loses weight and its hearing deteriorates. Older females like to be mothered, males are happier left in peace. As they're losing body fat, they seek warmth more and more.

Tips

- The ferret is a predator, but doesn't know how to devour its prey.
- Ferrets love hammocks.
- When a ferret spreads its toes, it's happy!
- Give ferrets dry cat food or special ferret food.
- Ferrets are highly motivated detectives.
- Never put sawdust in a ferret's cage!
- That infamous ferret smell will practically disappear after castration or sterilisation.
- Ferrets are clean animals by nature.
- But they do need some house-training.
- Never give a ferret aspirin!
- The 'war dance of the weasel' is a unique feature of the ferret.

- Ferrets are true escape artists.
- Young ferrets' teeth change at seven weeks. They then get double canine teeth.
- Being in season too long is life-threatening for a female!
- Buying a ferret needs to be carefully thought through.
- Contact with its own kind is vital for a ferret.
- Give a ferret plenty of time to get used to its new surroundings.

Useful addresses

Becoming a member of a club can be very useful for good advice and interesting activities. (Addresses and/or phone numbers may change in time.)

The Hants. & Berks. Ferret Club
http://www.hants.gov.uk/ferretclub/
Chairman: Derek Harding
Tel: 0118 9791260
e-mail: derek@pet-ferret.org.uk
N. Hampshire / Berkshire area

Ashfield Ferret Club of Nottingham
John Goddard
Tel: 0115 8548783
email: john@ashfieldferrets.co.uk
http://www.ashfieldferrets.co.uk/

North West Ferret Owners Club
Sec. Colin Sykes
http://www.redmap.co.uk/nwfoc/
email: committee@nwfoc.org

The Wessex Ferret Club
Southampton & South Hampshire area, England
General Inquiries Robin Tarrant
Tel: 02380 585421
Membership Secretary Jo Scott
Tel: 01980 610894
e-mail: am@power01.fsnet.co.uk
http://www.wessexferretclub.co.uk/index.htm

A ferret magazine
http://www.ferretsfirst.co.uk/

Other books from About Pets

- The Boxer
- The Border Collie
- The Cavalier King Charles Spaniel
- The Cocker Spaniel
- The Dalmatian
- The Dobermann
- The German Shepherd
- The Golden Retriever
- The Jack Russell Terrier
- The Labrador Retriever
- The Puppy
- The Rottweiler
- The Budgerigar
- The Canary
- The Cockatiel
- The Parrot
- The Lovebird
- The Cat
- The Kitten
- The Dwarf Hamster
- The Dwarf Rabbit
- The Gerbil
- The Guinea Pig
- The Hamster
- The Mouse
- The Rabbit
- The Rat
- The Goldfish
- The Tropical Fish
- The Snake

Key features of the series are:
- Most affordable books
- Packed with hands-on information
- Well written by experts
- Easy to understand language
- Full colour original photography
- 70 to 110 photos
- All one needs to know to care well for their pet
- Trusted authors, veterinary consultants, breed and species expert authorities
- Appropriate for first time pet owners
- Interesting detailed information for pet professionals
- Title range includes books for advanced pet owners and breeders
- Includes useful addresses, veterinary data, breed standards.

about pets

The Ferret

Name:	Ferret
Latin name:	*Mustela putorius furo*
Male:	Hob
Female:	Jill
Body length:	Hob: approx. 40 cm
	Jill: approx. 30 cm
Length of tail:	11 - 18 cm
Weight:	Hob: 1200 - 2500 g
	Jill: 800 - 1200 g
Number of teats:	8
Heart rate:	230 / minute
Body temperature:	38,5 - 38,8° C
Mating season:	March - August
Fertile:	from first season (8 - 9 months)
Gestation:	42 days
Number of young:	average 8 (max. 18)
Weight at birth:	7 - 10 g
Average life:	8 - 10 years